Thomas More

Over five hundred years ago,
at Christmas time, a play was
put on in an archbishop's palace
in London.

One of the archbishop's young
pages joined in and made
everyone laugh. The boy's
name was Thomas More.

This child will turn
out to be a
marvellous man.

Thomas's family was rich, but he worked in the archbishop's palace as a servant. This often happened at this time. Parents sent their children to an important

person's house to work, to learn proper manners and to make (they hoped) important friends. The children also carried on with their school lessons.

Thomas loved to joke and play, but he worked hard too. When he was about 14, he became a studen at Oxford University. There he studied Latin, as well as other subjects like maths and music. In those days people who could write used Latin as often as English.

After two years, Thomas
returned to London to train
as a lawyer.

Thomas wasn't sure what he wanted to do, though. He was very religious and, for a while, he thought about becoming a monk or a priest.

It would have been better not to marry – but I am weak.

But priests were not allowed
to marry then, and Thomas
wanted to get married. He and
his wife, Jane, had four children.
Then Jane died. Within a
month, Thomas married his
new wife, Alice.

Thomas loved his children dearly. He was kind to them, but strict too. He made them study hard, and write to him every day when he was away from home.

You educate your daughters too?

Thomas was strictest of all with himself. He spent many hours praying, and wore a rough hair shirt under his fine clothes. He tried to live a very holy life.

11

Thomas believed that people should spend every moment usefully. In his spare time, he wrote books and poems.
His book *Utopia* eventually made him famous all over Europe. He was known as one of the cleverest men in England.

Thomas was friends with other famous writers, too, including a Dutch priest called Erasmus.

Thomas was ambitious, and
with a big family to support
he needed to make money.
He was a brilliant lawyer.
Soon he became a judge, and
a member of Parliament as well.

The More
household

14

What Thomas really wanted to do, though, was to work for the king, Henry VIII. This was the best way to become powerful and rich – but it was also risky.

King Henry liked Thomas.
He was clever and he made
Henry laugh. Henry and his wife,
Catherine, often invited Thomas
to supper. Soon Thomas found
he hardly saw his family.

And when Thomas *was* at home, the king visited him – sometimes as a surprise.

At first, Thomas worked as a kind of secretary for Henry. Sometimes he made speeches welcoming important foreign visitors. He was also sent on royal missions abroad. In 1520 he went with Henry to a famous

meeting with the French king, François I, at the Field of the Cloth-of-Gold.

It was a crowded trip, though – Henry took 4,000 people in all.

Later, Thomas became Lord Chancellor, which meant he was one of Henry's most important ministers.

Thomas worked especially hard trying to stamp out new religious ideas that he thought were evil. He ordered books about these ideas to be burnt.

If the people who believed the ideas wouldn't change their minds, Thomas had them put in prison or put to death.

At this time, people all over
Europe were arguing about
the right way to worship God.
The people who stuck to the
old ways were called Catholics.
The people who had new ideas
were later called Protestants.

Like Thomas, King Henry hated most of the new ideas. Soon, though, Henry began to see that some of them might be useful in an argument he was having with the Pope.

Very interesting ...

23

This argument was about Henry's marriage. He wanted the Pope to say he could divorce Queen Catherine and marry someone else.

Henry asked Thomas what he thought about this idea. Thomas didn't agree with it, but he promised he wouldn't tell anyone else his opinion.

You'll come round to my way of thinking soon, Thomas. You'll see.

25

Years went by, and still the Pope couldn't decide whether to allow Henry's divorce or not. Henry was very angry.

Meanwhile, some people were saying that the Pope shouldn't be head of the Church.

Henry's ministers persuaded
Parliament to pass a law saying
that, instead, *Henry* was head
of the Church of England.
This meant he could judge the
divorce himself. Henry divorced
Catherine.

Thomas didn't want to be Henry's Lord Chancellor any more. He knew how dangerous it was for one of Henry's ministers to disagree with anything the king did. So he gave up the job.

Thomas told everyone it was because he wasn't well. All he wanted now was to live quietly with his family.

But Thomas was not allowed to live quietly. His enemies at court started spreading rumours.

Henry was worried. Many people disagreed with the changes he and his ministers were making to the Church. And he had heard that King Charles of Spain was planning to attack England. Henry thought these people might help Charles push him off the throne.

31

By this time Henry had married a new wife, Anne Boleyn. When she was crowned queen, Thomas was invited to the ceremony, but he stayed at home.

Anne was pregnant, and Henry was certain this baby would be the son he was longing for. He wanted to make sure that everyone agreed that this son should be the next king after him.

So Henry and his ministers decided that everyone had to swear an oath to say that they agreed with Henry's new marriage, and with all the changes he had made to the English Church.

What is it we're agreeing with?

The king's men travelled round the country, making everyone swear the oath. Anyone who refused was put in prison. Some were put to death.

Important people were called to swear the oath one by one. Soon it was Thomas's turn.

Thomas believed that if he swore an oath he disagreed with, he would go to hell. But he knew that Henry would be furious with him for not swearing. That night he lay awake, worrying about what would happen.

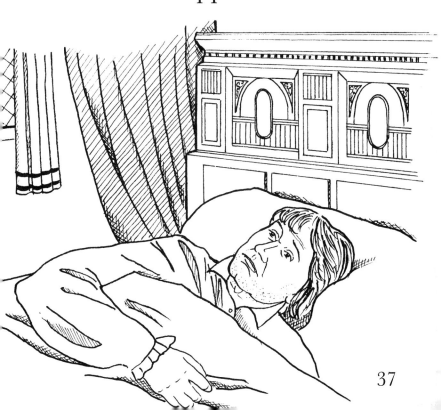

When the time came, Thomas was brave and calm. He said he was the king's loyal subject, but he would not swear the oath.

Some of Henry's ministers
thought Thomas should be
allowed to go home, if he
promised to keep quiet.
But Henry flew into a rage.
Thomas was locked up in the
Tower of London, and stayed
there for over a year.

Life in prison, Thomas thought,
was a bit like being a monk.
He spent his time reading
and writing and praying.

When at last Henry ordered his books to be taken away, Thomas was very upset. The man who came to take them was a lawyer called Richard Rich. He talked to Thomas, trying to make him explain why he wouldn't swear Henry's oath.

Finally, Thomas was put on trial. He was weak and ill, but he spoke bravely and cleverly.

Richard Rich told the judges that Thomas had said Henry

They have to find him guilty. It is the King's wish.

should not be head of the Church. A new law had been passed which meant you could be put to death for this. Rich was probably lying. Still, Thomas was found guilty.

Thomas was taken back to the Tower. His wife and children pushed through the crowds to hug and kiss him. His jailer burst into tears.

A few days later Thomas had his head chopped off. When King Henry was told the news, he was angry. He told Queen Anne that she had made him kill a good man.

Further facts

Anne Boleyn's baby

Henry VIII was certain that Anne Boleyn's baby would be a boy. He was wrong; Anne had a girl, called Elizabeth. Henry was furious – little did he know what a great and famous queen Elizabeth I would turn out to be. Soon Henry grew tired of Anne, and the year after Thomas More died, he had her head chopped off too.

Saint Thomas More

Today, the people who follow the ways of worshipping God

that Thomas More agreed with are called Roman Catholics. In 1935 the Roman Catholic Church decided to make Thomas a saint. This was because he always tried to live as holy a life as he could, and because he bravely chose to die rather than give up his beliefs.

A story for Shakespeare

One of the books Thomas More wrote was called *The History of Richard III.* Richard III had been the king of England when Thomas was a little boy, and Thomas thought he was a bad and cruel man. Many years after Thomas's death, William Shakespeare decided to write a play based on Thomas's story.

Some important dates in Thomas More's lifetime

1478 Thomas More is born in London.

about 1490 Thomas is sent to live in the household of John Morton, Archbishop of Canterbury.

about 1492 Thomas becomes a student at Oxford University.

about 1494 Thomas returns to London to train as a lawyer.

1505 Thomas marries Jane Colt. They have four children.

1511 Jane dies. Within a month, Thomas marries Alice Middleton.

1515 Thomas writes *Utopia*.

1518 Thomas starts working full-time for King Henry VIII.

1529 Thomas becomes Lord Chancellor.

1532 Thomas resigns as Lord Chancellor.

1533 Henry marries Anne Boleyn.

1534 Thomas is sent to the Tower of London.

1535 Thomas is executed

48